Too Cool For Drugs

Sharon Scott, L.P.C.

Wayne Hindmarsh, Ph.D.

With Nicholas, the Cocker Spaniel

Illustrated by George Phillips

HRD

HUMAN RESOURCE
DEVELOPMENT PRESS

Published by
Human Resource Development Press, Inc.
22 Amherst Road, Amherst, Massachusetts 01002
(413) 253-3488
1-800-822-2801 (U.S. and Canada)

ISBN 0-87425-236-9

In Loving Memory of Nicholas' Best Friend—

Shawn

August 5, 1979 – August 11, 1993

Other Books by Sharon Scott

Peer Pressure Reversal

How to Say No and Keep Your Friends

Too Smart for Trouble

Positive Peer Groups

When to Say Yes! And Make More Friends

Not Better... Not Worse... Just Different

Other Books by Dr. Wayne Hindmarsh

Drugs: What Your Kid Should Know

About the Authors

Wayne Hindmarsh, M.Sc., Ph.D., is currently Dean and Professor of Pharmacy at the University of Manitoba, Canada. Before joining academia, he spent time working in a crime detection laboratory for the Royal Canadian Mounted Police. He is President of PRIDE CANADA (Parent Resources Institute for Drug Education), a drug education and prevention organization that sponsors parent and youth groups across Canada, and has spoken on drug education to thousands at local, national, and international conferences throughout Canada, the United States, Australia, and Europe. In recognition of his involvement and his outstanding work in drug education, he received the Pharmacist of the Year award in Saskatchewan, Canada, and a meritorious service award from the Canadian Pharmaceutical Association. He was also honored with a commemorative medal from the Governor General of Canada.

Dr. Hindmarsh is the author of a parent handbook, *Drugs: What Your Kid Should Know*, and has written over 80 scientific research articles, primarily in the field of toxicology, as well as chapters in textbooks. He has been a guest on several Canadian radio and television talk shows, and is a frequent speaker for educational, health professional, and youth conferences.

Sharon Scott, M.A., is a licensed professional counselor and marriage and family therapist with 24 years' experience. As president of Dallas-based Sharon Scott and Associates, she travels worldwide to speak to students, parents, and educators on many topics. She has personally taught her Peer Pressure Reversal techniques to over three-quarters of a million people all across the United States,

Canada, Australia, Malaysia, and Micronesia. For seven years, she served as Director of the Dallas Police Department's First Offender Program. That program became a national model for delinquency prevention.

Ms. Scott has authored six other widely acclaimed books. She has been interviewed by numerous media, including CNN, *20/20, Good Morning Australia, USA Today,* TASS (the Russian news agency), *Teen Magazine,* and *The Washington Post.* She was honored by the Texas Counseling Association with the "Professional Writing Award," in St. Louis with the "Heart of America Award" for helping youth be drug-free, and by a Texas gubernatorial Certificate of Appreciation for her volunteer efforts in drug education.

Nicholas, Ms. Scott's Cocker Spaniel, is eight years old and has his D.O. (Dog Obedience) degree from Richland College. He is listed in the 1993 *Who's Who of Animals.* Nicholas also "co-authored" two other children's books with Ms. Scott: ***Too Smart for Trouble*** and ***Not Better... Not Worse... Just Different***. Nicholas frequently accompanies Ms. Scott to elementary schools. Since he was three months old, he has done volunteer work with the elderly at several nursing homes and with his homeless animal friends at the animal shelter.

Preface

If we wait until the teen years to teach our children to "say no to drugs," we may be too late. Young people are using drugs at an increasingly early age, and many children are offered drugs before they even enter their teens. For example, the average age at which youngsters are offered alcohol by their friends is eleven and a half years old! *Too Cool for Drugs* has been written for children who are at the elementary school level. Rather than simply telling them to say no to drugs, it recognizes that these children need to understand *why* and *how* to say no to drugs, and it equips them, chapter by chapter, with both the reasons and the methods for doing so. Because presenting this message in a way that will not scare them is so important, Nicholas the Cocker Spaniel has been chosen to make this serious subject fun to learn. Nicholas, with his childlike curiosity, shows children how to have a good time and "be cool" without the use of chemicals. Through his example, they learn how to open up to adults and ask questions about the drug-related problems they encounter; they also learn how to deal in a healthy way with the more difficult answers to their questions.

Some people think that all we have to do to help children avoid drugs is to teach them to say no and walk away. Although these people mean well, their thinking is based on naive assumptions; unfortunately, the situation isn't that simple. Generally, children are first offered drugs by a friend or relative. Afraid of being teased or of losing a friend, the best of children can make poor decisions. The addictive nature of many drugs may lead to frequent use and a habit that is difficult to break. Children feel an enormous need to be liked by others and to "fit in": the pressure to be accepted by their peers should never be treated lightly.

We are concerned that too many adults take a lax attitude toward the use of tobacco and alcohol by young people—these are drugs that can take a child's life. The excuses of "Boys will be boys" and "At least my child's not on 'real' drugs" are dangerous! We are saddened by the drug-related tragedies that we too often see in our workplace and long for a world of healthy drug-free people. We hope this book makes a strong contribution toward fulfilling that desire.

Many thanks to the following people who helped prepare this book:

- George Phillips for his delightful illustrations

- Lois Hindmarsh for assisting in field testing

- Michelle Cooper for typing the manuscript and assisting on photo shoots

- The HRD Press staff, including Nelda Jansen and Martha Cantwell, who "put it all together"

- The helpful young "editors" who made sure that the words we used weren't too big: David Carver, grade 4; Anne Strickland, grade 2; Evan Luck, grade 4; Ryann Matthisen, grade 5; Rachel Carver, grade 2; David Zacharias, grade 2; Lindsay Williams, grade 4; Andrew Strickland, grade 4; Benjamin Matthisen, grade 3; and Chelsea Williams, grade 2; and

- The darling children who appear on the book's cover: back row (left to right)—Cassidy Hill, grade 5; Michael Paul Brannon, grade 2; Allen Parkin, grade 5; and front row with Nicholas—Mariel Aquino, grade K.

And, of course, extra pats and hugs to Nicholas and his animal friends, Shawn, Mandy, Cedric, and Katy, who let their "mom" take hundreds of pictures of them to get one "just right."

Dallas, Texas   Sharon Scott
July 1993

Winnipeg, Canada   Wayne Hindmarsh
July 1993

An Important Note to Parents and Teachers

This book will be most effective for your child or student if you follow these suggestions:

1. First, read the book by yourself.

2. Then read it to, or with, the child. The comprehension of young children varies greatly, so you may need to elaborate on certain points to help the child understand them.

3. Slowly work through the book together, reading it in small amounts—no more than one chapter at a time. Then have some light discussion about what was read. You could have the children tell what they learned to another adult (such as a parent or teacher) or to their doll or dog.

4. Avoid lecturing while reading (e.g., "I hope you're listening to this. You'll need it." Or, "Remember when you smoked that cigarette with Billy? This book may help you keep from acting so dumb again.") Do not use the book to discipline. It should always be used on a positive note.

5. In Chapter 9, let the child answer (or act out) what he or she would say or do when offered drugs, *before* you read the next page about how the child in the story handled it. This gives the child an opportunity to think and to practice.

6. Read with enthusiasm and emotion in your voice— especially when Nicholas the Cocker Spaniel is relating a story. Both of you should have fun as you read.

Note to Teachers And Other Professional Helpers:

Teaching transparencies and a Nicholas puppet are available from HRD Press, Inc. Call or write for details (see page 120 for listing).

Table of Contents

Chapter 1
What Are Drugs?

Mom said, "Let's talk."

Hi! My name is Nicholas. I am an eight-year-old Cocker Spaniel. In case you do not know, a Cocker Spaniel is a kind of a dog.

Believe it or not, I'm a dog who writes books. In fact, this is the third book that I have written.

Let me tell you a little about myself. I have blonde hair and brown eyes.

My favorite activity is eating. My next favorite activities are playing with my toys and going for walks. What do you like to do for fun?

I live in Dallas, Texas, with my mom and dad. I have two brothers—Shawn, a Cocker Spaniel; and Cedric, an orange cat. I also have two sisters—Mandy, a terrier dog; and Katy, a calico kitten.

My mom, Sharon Scott, is a counselor. A counselor is a person who tries to help people with problems. She helped me (a little) in the writing of this book.

Mom said that I was old enough for a very important talk. She told me that we needed to talk about drugs.

"What are drugs?" I said.

She said that drugs are chemicals, or substances, that affect our body.

Mom said that some drugs are good for us. Good drugs are called medicine. They are given to us by doctors and nurses, or by our parents or other adult relatives. Good drugs help make us well when we are sick. For instance, if you have a bad cough, your mom might give you cough syrup to help you stop coughing.

I know about good drugs. My brother, Shawn, has an old, sick, and very tired heart. He goes to a dog doctor called a veterinarian. The vet gave Mom some medicine that she has to give Shawn two times every day. It has helped him a lot!

I told Mom to give him lots of the good medicine. I thought it would help him more. But she explained that you are supposed to take medicine the way that the doctor tells you to take it. The doctor writes how much medicine is needed (the dose) on a piece of paper called a prescription. Your parent takes the prescription to the pharmacy (or the drug store). The pharmacist fills the prescription exactly as the doctor ordered. Mom said it could make Shawn sicker to give him too much of the good medicine. So she will keep giving him the medicine two times every day as the vet told her.

Boy, I'm surely learning a lot!

Some drugs are bad for you. They hurt your body. You might not be able to think straight. Some drugs can cause you to pass out or to throw up. Yuck! Some drugs are so bad that they can even kill you.

Mom says that there are some people who take these bad drugs. They hurt their minds and their bodies.

I said, "Why would anyone make such a dumb decision?"

Mom said that usually people first try these bad drugs when they are with a buddy or a group of friends. Sometimes they are scared that their friends will tease them and call them names if they say "no" to drugs. They feel what is called peer pressure. Peer pressure is when someone close to your age tries to get you to do what they want you to do.

She said sometimes people try the bad drugs because they are curious. She said that trying these drugs even one time could get you "hooked." "Hooked" means that your body will want the drug again so badly that if it does not get the drug, then it will feel sick. So that causes the people to keep taking drugs.

"Wow, I would never want to get 'hooked' on drugs. So I'll never even try these bad drugs!"

Mom said that I was a really smart boy.

Mom said that someday someone will ask me to use some bad drugs.

"Will it be a mean person with a gun?" I asked.

Mom laughed and said, "No, Nicholas. That only happens on television! The person who asks you might be a neighbor whom you play with or a classmate." She said it might even be a relative. She also said sometimes people try to show off or look grown up by asking others to use drugs with them.

I think there are better ways to act grown up without asking people to use drugs, don't you?

Mom said, "Nicholas, tomorrow we are going to meet a man who is an expert on drugs. So make a list of any questions that you want to ask him."

Oh boy, I can't wait!

Dr. Wayne Hindmarsh
Drug Expert

Chapter 2
Meeting the Expert

Dr. Wayne welcomed me
to his office.

I was so excited!

I didn't think tomorrow would ever come, but it did. I had prepared my list of questions about drugs and was ready to ask the expert for some answers.

He welcomed us into his office. Mom said, "Nicholas, I want you to meet Dr. Wayne Hindmarsh. Dr. Hindmarsh, this is Nicholas."

"It is nice to meet you, Nicholas. Please call me Dr. Wayne."

Mom told him that I had some questions about drugs to ask him.

My first question was, "Where do you live, Dr. Wayne?" He said, "In Winnipeg, Canada. That is a long way from Texas, where you live, Nicholas."

I asked him, "How did you learn so much about drugs?" Dr. Wayne's answer was, "After I graduated from high school I went to the university for eight years. A lot of my classes were pharmacy classes. Pharmacy is learning about which drugs are good for people and which drugs are bad for people. It also teaches you how to take good drugs when you are ill and why you should never take bad drugs."

My third question was, "Why do some people sell those bad drugs?" Dr. Wayne said, "They think it's an easy way to make money. Sadly, they don't care how much the drugs hurt the people they sell them to. And sometimes the people who sell drugs are hooked on them. Their bodies now need these drugs, which cost them a lot of money. They don't think about or care about how it might hurt those who buy from them."

Next I asked him, "Do drugs hurt kids' bodies and grown-up bodies in the same way?" He said, "Drugs have a stronger effect on bodies that are still growing. That is why when the doctor or your parent gives you a good drug, medicine, the amount that you take is smaller than the amount a grown-up would take. And a bad drug will harm a child's body much quicker than it will hurt a grown-up's body."

My last question was, "What are the names of some drugs that are harmful?"

Dr. Wayne answered, "Tobacco, alcohol, marijuana (sometimes called 'pot' or 'grass'), inhalants, LSD, cocaine (sometimes called 'crack'), heroin, steroids, PCP, ecstasy, and speed."

I thanked Dr. Wayne for answering my questions. He told me to call him if I later thought of some more questions. I bet that I do!

Chapter 3
Puff, Puff...
Cough, Cough...

"What is this funny smelling creature?"

Our thanks to Connie Smith, The Birthday Farm, Rockwall, Texas, for letting Nicholas meet Major T.

I did not think that I would need to talk to Dr. Wayne again so soon. But here is what happened to me only two days after I visited with him.

Mom said, "Let's go visit our friends who live on the farm."

I was ready in a jiffy! I like to go to the farm.

When we got there, Mom went in the house to talk to her friends. I stayed outside to play. On the farm were chickens, cows, horses, and even pigs. Then around the corner of the barn came... what *is* it? And *it* smells funny.

A llama! I had never seen a llama before. The llama said, "Welcome to my farm. Who are you?"

I told him that my name was Nicholas and asked what his name was. He said, "Lou. Lou Llama."

He asked if I wanted to go play down at the creek. That sounded like fun, so off we went.

That's when it happened. He said, "Hey, Nicholas. Do you want to smoke?"

I asked, "Smoke what?"

"Don't act silly," he said, "A cigarette, man. Be cool."

Then I knew where the yucky smell was coming from.

He said, "Everybody smokes."

I told him that my mother, my father, my grandparents, and my brothers and sisters do not smoke.

He said, "What do they know? Don't be a baby."

I left Lou Llama at the creek to play by himself. I went straight back to the farmhouse. Mom was ready to go.

When we got in the car I told Mom that Lou Llama had tried to get me to smoke a cigarette. When she found out that I had said "no" to him, she said, "Nicholas, I'm so proud of you. You are smart. And you're **Too Cool** for drugs!"

Mom asked if I knew why I should not smoke cigarettes. I said, "I'm not sure. They're bad for your health, aren't they?"

She said, "Why don't you call Dr. Wayne and see what he can tell you about tobacco."

As soon as I got home, I called Dr. Wayne and told him about Lou Llama's offer. He said, "Nicholas, you made an excellent decision. Let me tell you why you should never use tobacco, whether it is in the form of a cigarette, a cigar, or the kind some people chew."

This is what Dr. Wayne told me.

"Have you ever seen the warning labels on cigarette packages? They say things like:

Warning: Smoking causes lung cancer, heart disease, emphysema, and may complicate pregnancy.

---

or

Warning: Cigarette smoke contains carbon monoxide.

---

or

Warning: Quitting smoking now greatly reduces serious risks to your health.

"Smoking is *not* cool. In fact, cigarettes can kill!"

He said, "Each cigarette contains hundreds of chemicals. Let's look at some of these chemicals:

1. *Nicotine*. When you smoke, this chemical gets into your blood as quick as a flash of lightening. This causes your heart to beat faster. Your veins get smaller, so less blood gets to the tip of your toes and the top of your head (where your brain is!). This is not good.

2. *Carbon monoxide*. Part of the cigarette when smoked turns into a gas. This gas joins part of your blood. This means there is less oxygen in your blood. You need oxygen to think clearly, do well in sports, and even to look good!

3. *Tar.* This black gooey chemical caused by smoking gets
    into your lungs. This causes you to cough and
    sometimes spit up yucky stuff. Healthy lungs should be
    pink. The lungs of a smoker are black because they are
    full of tar. Gross!

4. *Cancer-causing chemicals.* Many chemicals in
    cigarettes and chewing tobacco cause cancer. Cancer is
    a very serious disease. You can get cancer of the lung,
    throat, and mouth from using tobacco."

Dr. Wayne continued, "There is another type of smoking besides the one that goes into the body of the person smoking. This is called 'secondhand' smoke. Secondhand smoke comes from a cigarette burning in an ashtray or from a cigarette held by a smoker. The smoke goes into other people's bodies. Both kinds of smoke are bad for you.

"Secondhand smoke makes some people sneeze, gives them headaches, and causes their eyes to water. They are allergic to the smoke. Some people are so allergic that they will have trouble breathing. They might even have to go to the hospital.

"Some of you might live with an adult who smokes. You might be worried that smoking will make them sick. You might want to share with them what you have learned. But remember, adults have to make their own choices. It is very hard to quit once you have started smoking. Since you haven't started, you have the chance to make the right decision."

I told Dr. Wayne, "I don't know why anyone would want to smoke cigarettes. It makes you look bad—like a chimney with smoke pouring out!"

He agreed with me and said, "You also smell bad because the smoke gets in your hair and clothes. Your breath stinks, and tobacco stains your teeth. Your skin wrinkles faster. You can't taste food as well. And lots of people don't want to sit near you because of the bad smell. When you are older you will learn that some people won't date people who smoke because of the smell."

I told Dr. Wayne that I am never going to smoke. Mom told me about my grandfather who had to have heart surgery because he used to smoke. And she said that I had three other relatives who died because they got cancer from smoking cigarettes.

I told Dr. Wayne that I had better ways of spending money without burning it up smoking cigarettes. For what it costs to smoke one pack of cigarettes a day for one year, a person could buy five color TVs, ten VCRs, 55 Nintendo® games, or over 1,100 ice cream cones! Dr. Wayne said I was **Too Cool**!

I decided that I would write a letter to Lou Llama and tell him what I had learned about cigarettes. He seemed like a nice llama. I wondered whether anyone had ever told him how harmful cigarettes are. Here is my letter:

September 1, 1993

Lou Llama

Down On the Farm

Dear Lou Llama,

It was nice to meet you. Thank you for showing me the creek.

I am worried about you. Did you know that smoking is bad for your health? Dr. Wayne, my drug expert, told me that cigarettes have lots of bad chemicals in them. Some of those chemicals are the same as the ones in bug spray, the exhaust from a car, and asphalt which makes roads. Sounds good, huh? Bleaugh!

Please quit smoking. I want you to stay healthy so we can play again.

Your Friend,

Nicholas

Chapter 4
Stinkin' Drinkin'

"Boring commercial! It wants
Cedric, Shawn, and me to think
you have to drink alcohol to be cool."

The following week, while I was watching television with my brothers, Shawn and Cedric, I told them what Dr. Wayne had taught me about tobacco. They both said they would never in a million years start smoking cigarettes. I was glad they made such good decisions.

We quietly watched television for awhile, until a commercial came on advertising beer. Cedric, who is only five years old, asked, "What's beer?"

Shawn, being almost 14 years old, knew. He said that it was an alcoholic drink used by some adults. Shawn told us that he once found an open beer can lying in an alley and that it smelled funny.

The commercial showed people at a party having fun while they were drinking beer. Just then, Mom came into the room. She said, "Don't believe everything you see in commercials or read in advertisements!"

"Huh? Isn't everything true if it's on TV or in a magazine?"

Mom started laughing… really loudly!

Mom said that the alcohol company pays the television station or the magazine to advertise, or to sell, their alcohol. They make the commercial or advertisement look really good because they want lots of people to buy the alcohol. That way they make a lot of money. She said some people think that to have fun, they must drink. She said they must be really boring if they can't think of something fun to do besides drinking alcohol.

Mom said she has asked thousands of people what they thought about the taste of alcohol the first time they tried it. She said most of them say, "Yuck!" or "Gross!" or "It was bitter!" She then asked the people what food they really hated to taste. Some said they didn't like asparagus, some people didn't like liver, and some people didn't like broccoli. Everyone could name some food they did not like. She asked if they would ever try the food they didn't like again. They all yelled, "No way!"

When we taste a food we don't like, most of us will never ever try it again. Many will try alcohol and most will hate it. But many will try it again… and again. Why? Because their friends do. Or because someone told them it was a grown-up thing to do. Peer pressure again.

Nothing that you smoke or drink or eat can make you cool. *You*, your personality, is what makes you cool!

Mom said, "There are different kinds of alcohol, such as beer, wine, whiskey, vodka, gin, and malt liquor. Why don't you call Dr. Wayne and see what an expert can tell you about alcohol?"

And that's what we did. Cedric and Shawn got on an extension phone so they could listen to the conversation, too.

Dr. Wayne said that he was glad we called.

First, he told us a true story about a 10-year-old boy. The boy called to his dad from the bathroom. When his father walked in, he found his son acting in a strange way. The boy was sleepy and mixed-up, and he had bubbly spit coming from his mouth. His father rushed him to the hospital. It was learned that he had drunk a large amount of alcohol. The doctors had to "pump" his stomach to get the alcohol out of his body. That means the doctors put a long, thin tube down the boy's throat into his stomach to bring the alcohol out. I bet that was not fun!

Dr. Wayne said the boy had forgotten that alcohol is a chemical that affects how your body works. It is a drug. And it can be bad for your health and personality.

Dr. Wayne asked us, "Did you know that alcohol affects just about every part of your body? Some of these parts are the brain, liver, stomach, intestines, heart, and nerves.

"Alcohol slows down the brain. Alcohol is a depressant. That means a person cannot think as clearly as he should. The speed of his movements is slowed down. This is why it is so dangerous to drink and drive. Did you know that the reason why most teenagers die is because they drink and drive?"

Shawn said, "I'm almost old enough to get my driver's license. I'll *never* drink and drive. In fact, I don't plan to drink when I'm *not* driving."

Dr. Wayne told us that he used to work in a laboratory for the Royal Canadian Mounted Police. His job was to figure out the cause of automobile crashes in which someone had died. Most of the time, alcohol was the reason.

Dr. Wayne also said, "Scientists have found that alcohol slows the growth of your brain. So, if you drink a lot as a young person, it will take longer to act like an adult."

I said, "Some adults act like kids!"

Dr. Wayne replied, "That might be because they used to get drunk a lot when they were kids."

small brain

Alcohol

"Dr. Wayne, don't some people drink to try to fit in?" I asked. "They think that it makes them look cool."

He said, "You are right. Here are some things alcohol does to the way you look. We will start at your head and go down the body:

1. It makes the white part of your eyes turn red.

2. Your vision blurs.

3. You might say or do something you did not want to say or do.

4. You will have a terrible headache after you drink.

5. Your face may 'flush' or turn red.

6. You might get sleepy and drool.

7. A lot of people act silly when drinking.

8. You might pass out.

9. Some people act ugly and want to fight.

10. You might barf on your friends. Yuck!

11. You can get dizzy.

12. You will have to go to the bathroom a lot more.

13. Your body will get a lot of fattening calories, but no vitamins.

14. You can have trouble with your balance and you might bump into things.

15. You could die. (When too much alcohol goes into your body too quickly, it can poison your body.)"

"But Dr. Wayne, don't some adults drink?"

"Yes, Nicholas, they do. It is against the law to drink alcohol until you are grown up because, remember, alcohol can do more harm to a body that is still growing. It is legal to drink at a certain age. In some places, you need to be 21 years of age to drink. In other places, you are allowed to drink, if you want to, at age 18."

When I get close to the legal age to drink—which will be 13 more years—I'm going to do a lot more reading about alcohol. I want to make a good, healthy decision for my mind and body. I think I'm a nice-looking dog. I don't want to mess myself up by drinking. I bet I'll never drink alcohol at all. I'm **Too Cool**.

Chapter 5
Don't Be a Dope

Watching Wally, a drug detection dog, sniff out marijuana at the airport.

We appreciate the efforts of Officer Jim Hughes and his partner, Wally, who are assigned to the Drug Enforcement Administration Narcotics Task Force at DFW Airport. They have recovered $18 million in drug money and $400 million in illegal drugs in the past six years.

One day I was talking to Mom about what I want to be when I grow up. She said that I might want to be a drug detection dog.

"What is a drug detection dog?" I asked.

Mom said, "They are dogs trained to sniff out marijuana or other drugs. A lot of them work at airports and smell the luggage that comes off airplanes. Some people try to sneak these drugs that are against the law into our country. They want to try to make money by selling the drugs."

I said, "That is really mean because I know that marijuana is really bad for your health."

Mom asked, "Do you know what marijuana does to your body that makes it so bad?"

"Not really," I replied.

Mom said, "Why don't you…"

"I know. Call Dr. Wayne!"

"Dr. Wayne," I said, "a dog friend of mine, Wally, sniffs out marijuana at the airport. He paws any piece of luggage that has marijuana inside it. Then the person who owns the luggage is arrested. What is marijuana?"

"Nicholas, marijuana is actually a plant," he explained. "Some people take the leaves and roll them in paper. It looks sort of like a cigarette. A marijuana cigarette is called a 'joint.'

"The marijuana plant has over 400 chemicals in its leaves. When a person lights a joint, those 400 chemicals change into 2,000 chemicals. When a person smokes a joint, it is almost like taking 2,000 different pills at one time! We know a lot about one of those chemicals. It is called THC. I often call it **The Horrible Chemical.**

T.H.C. = The Horrible Chemical

"The THC in the marijuana likes fat. Our brains have a lot of fat in them. So guess where a lot of the horrible chemical goes? Yes, to our brain. And it stays there for a very long time. In fact, you can have marijuana in your body for up to 28 days after smoking just one joint!

"Nicholas, I know that you know how important your brain is. It is like a master computer. Without a brain, you couldn't think, walk, or talk. The brain is made up of billions of cells. These cells have bridges between them. Doctors call those bridges 'synapses.' In a healthy brain, the synapses are open and clear. That way your thoughts can travel easily from cell to cell.

Don't mess up your computer!

"But in the brain of a person who smokes marijuana, the bridges get full of THC. They stretch and become larger. When the thoughts of the person try to go across the bridge, it is more difficult for them to reach the other side. And it takes longer, so your thinking is slowed down. Most students' grades go down when they smoke marijuana. Most athletes don't run as fast. And musicians don't read their music as quickly. In fact, a nickname for marijuana is 'dope.' Why do you think they call it dope?"

"Gee," I said, "I'm never going to smoke marijuana. I don't want to become a dope!"

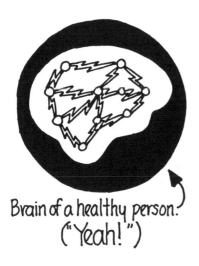

Brain of a healthy person.
("Yeah!")

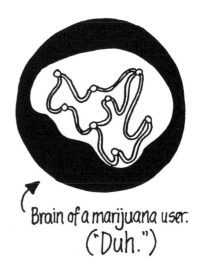

Brain of a marijuana user.
("Duh.")

"But that's not all, Nicholas. Marijuana also does harm to other parts of your body. THC does horrible things to your liver, to your lungs, and even to your heart.

"And, like cigarettes, marijuana joints have carbon monoxide gas, the black gooey stuff called tar, and other bad things. Smoking one joint does as much harm to the body as smoking at least five cigarettes! Smoking that stuff could cause breathing problems, and you might get cancer at a young age. Cancer of the lung, mouth, tongue, and neck have happened in some young people who smoke marijuana. Marijuana smoking also makes it harder to fight off infections. This means that the person will get more colds and flu."

I asked Dr. Wayne how much THC is in marijuana. He said that there are different amounts in each joint. Some of the joints have so much that they can cause all the bad things to happen even faster. He said that you cannot tell how much THC is in the joint by looking at it.

Dr. Wayne also said, "If you want to look cool, don't smoke marijuana! The muscles in boys' arms and chests won't grow like they should when they are teenagers. They will have weak-looking bodies."

I told Dr. Wayne that I had lots of muscles under all my hair!

He added, "Marijuana smoke smells funny—like a rope burning. So the smell gets into the person's hair and clothes. And your eyes get red."

That does it! No marijuana *ever* for me. I don't want to smell like a stinky rope on fire. I'm **Too Cool** for that!

Chapter 6
The Nose "No's"

Dad warned Katy, Mandy and me about the dangers of smelling fumes.

Mom said she was so proud of how much I was learning about drugs that she and Dad were going to take me to the park. She said that Dad needed to finish mowing the grass first.

My sisters, Mandy and Katy, and I were in the garage just messing around. Mandy said, "What's that smell?"

I told her it was the gasoline can. Dad would have to put gasoline in the lawn mower to get the motor to run. Katy walked over and started to smell the can.

I said, "No Katy! Smelling strong fumes like gasoline fumes is bad for our bodies." Katy is only one year old. She didn't know any better.

I told Mom that we could not go to the park. There was something more important to do.

Mom said, "Nicholas, besides eating, what is more important for you to do?"

"Taking care of my baby sister, Katy," I said. "She needs to learn about inhalants!"

And off we went to call Dr. Wayne.

"Dr. Wayne, I'm so glad you are in!" I exclaimed. "My baby sister, Katy, was sniffing the gasoline can. She doesn't know that it is dangerous. It could even kill her!"

Dr. Wayne said, "Nicholas, you are so right. Katy, let me tell you what inhalants are. 'Inhale' means to breathe in. So inhalants are chemical gases that are breathed in through the nose. You should never try to inhale or sniff fumes. In fact, the only thing you should ever try to sniff into your nose is nasal spray or nose drops that your doctor, parent, or other adult relative has given you. What needs to go in our noses is clean, fresh air that has oxygen that is good for our bodies."

Dr. Wayne told Katy that gasoline is only good for motors to breathe, such as lawn mowers or car engines. He said inhaled chemicals go straight to the brain. They make the person dizzy, drool, throw up, lose balance, see with blurred vision or see double, speak unclearly, fall down, and maybe become unconscious. A person might even die the first time he or she inhales chemicals.

He said that the bad chemicals in inhalants not only can hurt your brain but also can hurt your liver, your kidneys, and all your nerves. Dr. Wayne said, "I've also heard of boys and girls who have suffered serious heart damage from using inhalants. Their heart began beating so quickly that it couldn't fill up with blood. And the heart needs to be full of blood so that it can pump blood to all the parts of the body."

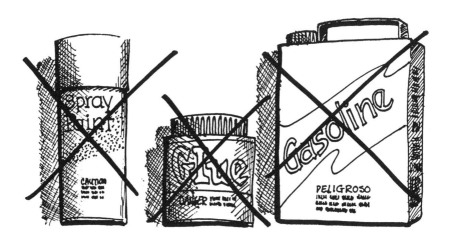

Dr. Wayne told Katy, "If anyone ever tries to get you to smell, sniff, inhale, huff, or breathe in something through your nose, *don't* do it! And talk to your parent about it."

Katy said, "I'm never going to sniff anything except fresh air."

I told her that since she's a girl it would be okay to smell perfume. But she shouldn't put it *in* her nose to breathe it!

She told me not to be silly. I'm not silly. I'm **Too Cool**! And I'm going to show you 101 ways that you can be **Too Cool**, too!

Chapter 7
Too Cool, Too!

There are so many ways to
have fun—like playing on a gym set!

It is important for all of us to have lots of fun things to do. And doing drugs is *not* fun. There are lots of ways to be cool. Here are 101 ways that I've thought of to be cool:

1. Jump rope.

2. Go swimming.

3. Walk your dog. (Remember to put his leash on!)

4. Learn to play tennis.

5. Travel to another country by reading a book about it.

6. Plant some flower seeds or grow a tomato plant.

7. Write down on a calendar the birthdays of your friends and relatives so that you remember to send them a birthday card.

8. Ice-skate.

9. Memorize a poem.

10. Learn to sew.

11. Make a model car.

12. Paint a picture.

13. Play hopscotch.

14. Have a friend sleep over.

15. Learn to cook something special, like brownies or pizza.

16. Build a tree house.

17. Learn a craft.

18. Play dominoes.

19. Feed ducks at a nearby park.

20. Join scouts.

21. Play marbles.

22. Pitch horseshoes.

23. Run races with friends.

24. Pop popcorn.

25. Build a bird house.

26. Go jogging.

27. Build a snow fort (or a cardboard fort).

28. Play soccer.

29. Make a list of ways your family can recycle.

30. Fly a kite.

31. Plant a tree.

32. Decorate an orange juice can to use as a pencil holder.

33. Have a magic show.

34. Use the dictionary to learn one new word each day.

35. Donate a warm blanket to a shelter for the homeless.

36. Go to a garage sale (or have one).

37. Get some posters from a travel agency to decorate your room.

38. Play hockey.

39. Listen to music.

40. Shovel or sweep a driveway for an elderly neighbor.

41. Join a boy's or girl's club.

42. Play croquet.

43. Play tag.

44. Go horseback riding.

45. Mow lawns or pull weeds for spending money.

46. Have a stamp or rock collection.

47. Get a book on birds and bird watch.

48. Plant a vegetable garden.

49. Visit a nursing home and brighten someone's day.

50. Play checkers.

51. Call your grandparent.

52. Cross-country or downhill ski (if there is snow!).

53. Go skateboarding or rollerblading.

54. Have a friend over to play games.

55. Pet your cat.

56. Play Nintendo® or other video games.

57. Read a funny comic book.

58. Work a crossword puzzle.

59. Go to a park and swing.

60. Play softball.

61. Window-shop.

62. Take your old toys to a place that will give them to needy children.

63. Think about what you want to make your parent for Mother's or Father's Day.

64. Learn the names of the trees and plants in your yard.

65. Make a get-well card for someone who is sick.

66. Play with your dolls or other toys.

67. Wash your parent's car.

68. Straighten your closet.

69. Play with Lego.®

70. Go on a picnic.

71. Adopt a homeless pet from an animal shelter.

72. Play charades.

73. Put together a jigsaw puzzle.

74. Play basketball or football.

75. Rake leaves.

76. Color in a coloring book.

77. Help a friend with a chore.

78. Visit a relative.

79. Have a lemonade stand.

80. Make candy with your mother.

81. Look at your family photo albums (or put pictures in an album).

82. Play miniature golf.

83. Clean your room. (Surprise your parent!)

84. Do your homework first thing when you get home so you can relax.

85. Ride your bike and feel the fresh air on your face.

86. If it's spring, put some short pieces of string outside for the birds to use to build their nests.

87. Bake cookies.

88. Watch the stars at night.

89. Count fireflies in your yard.

90. Take turns telling your friends about your favorite holiday or trip.

91. Bathe your dog. (We like to be clean too!)

92. Play hide-and-seek.

93. Make homemade ice cream (or go buy yogurt).

94. Sing songs.

95. Visit a friend and help them finish their homework.

96. Look at your clothes and see how you can mix and match them to make different outfits.

97. Write a letter to an old friend.

98. Go tobogganing or sleigh riding (if you live where there is lots of snow!).

99. Learn to play the piano or other musical instrument.

100. Learn the history of the flag of your country.

101. Teach your best friend what you learned in this book.

What can you add to the list to be **Too Cool**, too? Write down your ideas:

1. _____

2. _____

3. _____

4. _____

5. _____

Keep a record of which of these **Too Cool** fun ideas you try!

Chapter 8
Winners Call
Their Own Shots

Always think like a winner!

Remember Lou Llama and how he tried to talk me into smoking cigarettes? He even called me some names. And remember the advertisements and commercials that try to make things like alcohol look good so that we will buy them? They try to make us think that we won't be macho, or pretty, or cool if we don't use their product.

So it's important to think like a winner. Feel good about yourself! That way other kids and commercials can't pressure us. Each of us needs to have so much confidence that we always do our own thinking. We do what is best for us.

Here are 12 ways to help build your confidence:

1. Every day write down in a notebook something you did that day that you are proud of or feel good about.

2. Select friends who are nice people. They should be polite, follow rules, and treat others nicely. I also hope they treat animals well, too.

3. Keep yourself in good shape. Eat lots of fruits and vegetables. Try not to eat a lot of sugar or fried foods. Try to exercise at least 12 minutes every day. You could walk, ride your bicycle, skip, play kickball, swim, stretch, or jump rope.

4. Write a history of your family. Ask your parent or guardian about where they came from. And talk to your grandparents about where they are from. I bet you have a lot of special relatives.

5. Read good books about people who have worked hard to reach their goals. Ask your teacher or librarian at your school for some ideas.

6. Do something kind every day. Say "hi" to someone who is lonely, be a good listener, and be helpful. Helping others makes us all feel good.

7. Make a list of *how* you are smart. Everyone is smart but in different ways. Some people are good at being quiet and listening. Some people are smart at math. Other people are good at spelling. Some people are good at giving a report in front of the class. Other people are good at music or playing a sport. Some people are good at thinking and solving problems. Some people are smart because of how nice they always are. Some people are good at being friends with animals. Other people are smart because they are always on time. How are you smart?

8. Make friends with an elderly person in your neighborhood or in a nursing home. Think of ways that you could help them or have fun together. Helping others makes us feel good about ourselves.

9. Dream about what you want to be when you grow up. Talk to someone who does that work. Find out why they like it. Ask them what they had to do to become what they are.

10. Think of something that you really enjoy. Think of ways that you might get better at it. Write down your goal in a notebook. Your goal might be to read four books during the summer, or swim farther, or get better at math. Then write in your notebook how you are doing.

11. If some of your friends tease others in unkind ways, don't join in. It is better to notice something good about the person they are putting down. This way you will have a winning personality.

12. Think about some peer pressure situations that might happen to you some day. Decide now what you could say or do to get out of them. By doing this, you will be prepared if anyone ever asks you to steal or to cheat or to use drugs.

Chapter 9
It's Cool
To "No" Your Way

Mom said, "Nicholas, 'looking pitiful' is not a good way to say 'no' to drugs. I'll teach you some better ways."

One day I was eating my favorite snack, oranges, in the kitchen. I asked Mom what I should do if someone came up to me with a gun and tried to make me use drugs.

She laughed and said, "Nicholas, remember I said that's not the way it will happen. People who ask you to use drugs will almost always be people whom you know. It might be a friend from school who wants you to smoke a cigarette. It could be a cousin visiting us who asks you to smoke marijuana. It might be when you are at a sleepover that a friend wants you to sneak some wine out of the refrigerator."

"Oh," I said. "I don't want to lose my friends. So what do I say or do to keep from going along with them?"

Mom said, "That's a good question, Nicholas. I'm going to teach you five different ways to turn down drugs. And you won't lose friends, either. In fact, *real* friends won't drop you when you make your own decisions. The worst thing that could happen is that they might be mad at you for a few hours or a day.

"There is one kind of friend whom you might need to lose, though. If your friend *keeps* using drugs, you should select a better friend. Because if you keep hanging out with them, two bad things could happen. You might be with them when they are caught and get into trouble. Or they might finally pressure you to give in and do drugs with them."

I told Mom that I surely did not want that to happen.

She said, "Let's sit down and learn what to say or do when friends offer you drugs."

1. Just Say No

Sometimes you can just say, "No." But you have to say it by looking straight at the person. And you have to have a firm voice. You have to look like you mean what you say. Don't be rude or mean, but be strong.

There are many ways to say no. Here are a few:

"No!"

"No thanks."

"That's wrong."

"Surely you know better."

"Nope to dope."

"Forget it!"

"No way, Jose."

Shake your head no.

"I'm not interested."

"Never in a million years."

If you have said no twice, and your friend is still pressuring you, then you must...

2. Leave

Walk away from the trouble. Go play somewhere else, a place that is safe. Or go home. Call home for a ride if you need to.

You don't have to walk away mad or stuck up. You should not walk away scared. Walk away normally. Look proud. Your eyes should look straight ahead.

And don't do the "yo-yo"! That is when you walk away at first but then keep coming back to them as they talk to you more. You are acting just like a yo-yo. If you take too long getting out of trouble, it gives them more time to pressure you. So be quick. It is best to get out of trouble in 30 seconds or less. That is about the length of a commercial on television.

3. Make a Joke

Another way to say no is silly and quite funny. Say no in joking ways. Your friends will laugh, but they will also know that you are serious about not doing drugs.

Here are some ways to say no to drugs by using joking lines:

"I can't. I've got to go floss my cat's teeth."

"Can't. I've got my totem pole carving class tonight."

"Too busy. I've got to wash my underwear."

"No thanks. My lungs are into fresh air today."

"No, I've got to get home. I'm expecting a call from the man in the moon."

"I've already said yes too many times today. It's time for me to say no."

"I've already bought a ticket to ride Aladdin's magic carpet."

"I'm too busy. I'm attending the opening of my garage door."

"Sorry. I promised my gerbil that I would rollerblade with him."

"If I used that stuff, I would forget where I parked my brain!"

Can you think of other joking ways to say no to drugs?

4. Better Idea

Help yourself and your friend, too, by coming up with a better idea. Think of something fun to do that you know your friend can't pass up. Look at the list of 101 ways to be cool in Chapter 7 for ideas on what you could suggest. And it is very important to walk toward the better idea when you suggest it. Then you look serious. And your friend will probably follow you. Just make sure that they don't bring any drugs with them! They need to throw the drugs in a trash can if they are going to play with you. Tell them not to leave the drugs on the ground because younger children could find them and get sick if they put the drugs in their mouths.

A better idea sounds like this:

🐾 "Let's do _____ instead."

🐾 Or, "I've got a better idea. It would be fun to ___."

Can you fill in the blanks?

Cool people can always think of better things to do.

Nicholas

chicken

5. Return the Dare

Sometimes people may tease you and call you names if you don't do drugs with them. They are trying to show off. And when you won't let them boss you around, they might call you a name.

If someone calls you a "chicken" or a "baby," don't say, "No, I'm not," or "Darers go first." Those lines don't work.

What you need to do is **Return the Dare**. It is like playing ball. When someone throws a ball to you, you throw it back. Well, when someone dares you, put the dare back on them.

When someone calls you a "chicken," you could return the dare by saying:

🐾 "If I'm the chicken, then you're the egg."

🐾 "I'd rather be a chicken than a dead duck."

🐾 You could sing, "I feel like chicken tonight," or you could:

🐾 Pretend to pluck a feather from your arm and hand it to them as you walk away.

🐾 Flap your wings and cluck like a chicken as you leave.

When someone says, "If you're my friend, you'll smoke (or drink) this with me," then you could say:

🐾 "If you were my friend, you would get off my back."

🐾 Or, "I *am* your friend and that is why I'm not going to do it with you."

"Gosh, Mom, I didn't know there were so many ways to turn down drugs," I said.

Mom also said, "Be sure you tell me or another adult whom you trust if someone offers you drugs."

Mom told me that these ways to say no could be used when I'm asked to do *any* kind of trouble. She said if someone asks me to steal, then I should leave. And if someone wants my homework, I could suggest a better idea. I could say, "I'm not going to give you my paper to cheat with. But the next time you don't understand your homework, call me at home and maybe we can study together."

Wow, I know so much more about saying no to drugs and other trouble! Don't you? We are **Too Cool for Drugs**!

Mom said she wants to tell me some stories. She wants me to practice what I have learned. Are you ready to help me?

Jessica's Story

Jessica and Stephanie were riding the school bus home. As soon as they got off the bus, Stephanie whispered to Jessica, "Guess what I've got? A cigarette. Let's smoke it while we walk home."

Before you read the next page, answer what you would say or do if you were Jessica:

_____

_____

_____

Jessica's Decision

Jessica said, "No, don't you know how harmful cigarettes are? Some of the chemicals in cigarettes, like tar and carbon monoxide, do terrible things to your lungs and heart."

Stephanie said, "All the movie stars smoke!"

Jessica said, "Most don't. Smoking wrinkles your skin. And a lot of the movie stars who smoked, like John Wayne and Sammy Davis, Jr., have died from lung cancer. Besides, I do what is smart for me, not for someone else. And if you're going to smoke it, you can't walk with me because it stinks." Jessica began quickly walking home.

That is when Stephanie said, "Wait. You're right. I'm sorry." The girls walked home together.

Jessica Said No And Left.

Joshua's Story

Joshua and Paul are friends from school. One day they were shooting baskets in the park. It was hot so they stopped for a short rest. That's when Paul saw the beer can.

Paul said, "Joshua, look at this empty beer can." Then he picked it up and said, "Hey it's not empty! There is still some beer in it. Let's taste it."

Before you read the next page, answer what you would say or do if you were Joshua:

_____

_____

_____

Joshua's Decision

Yesterday at school, Joshua had heard a guest speaker tell about the harm that drinking alcohol can do to your body, so he was ready with his answer. "No way," he said. "Alcohol slows down your brain so you might say or do something that you don't want to do. And it can make you act weird. Some people get really sleepy, some people fight, and some people barf after drinking alcohol. And I don't want to do any of that. Count me out."

Paul said, "Gosh, I wish I hadn't been sick and missed school yesterday. What else did the guest speaker say?"

"Lots," said Joshua. They spent the next hour talking about it. And Joshua helped his friend Paul learn about why he shouldn't drink alcohol.

Joshua Said No And Had A Better Idea.

Ashley's Story

Ashley and her parents were just finishing cooking lots of food. They were having the family reunion at their house. Ashley was so excited that her favorite teenage cousin, Eric, was coming to visit.

Finally, everyone arrived. The meal was delicious. Ashley asked Eric if he would like to see their new colt. Off they went.

After looking at the colt, Eric pulled something from his pocket and lit it.

Ashley said, "That cigarette sure smells funny."

"It's a joint," Eric laughed. "You want to try it?"

Before you read the next page, answer what you would say or do if you were Ashley:

_____

_____

_____

Ashley's Decision

Ashley was lucky because her parents had talked to her about drugs. She knew that marijuana has hundreds of harmful chemicals, especially THC. She remembered that the THC fills the bridges between the brain cells, slowing down thinking. She also thought that maybe this was why Eric's eyes were so red and why he had a cold.

Ashley said, "No thanks, Eric. That stuff is really bad for you. That's why it's against the law. I wish you would quit."

Eric said, "Yeah, someday. Maybe."

After all the relatives left, Ashley told her parents what had happened. She knew Eric needed help. Ashley's parents were pleased that she handled the situation so well.

Ashley Said No And Told An Adult Whom She Trusted.

Roberto's Story

Roberto and Carlos were putting together a model airplane. When they started gluing the parts together, Carlos said, "This glue smells good." He held it up for Roberto to smell.

Before you read the next page, answer what you would say or do if you were Roberto:

_____

_____

_____

Roberto's Decision

Roberto said, "Don't do that. Don't you know that sniffing is dangerous?"

Carlos said, "What are you talking about?"

Roberto told Carlos that sniffing chemicals like gasoline, paint, or glue was so dangerous that it could kill you. He told Carlos never to put these things close to his nose. Roberto said, "Read the instructions on these products. You will see that these products *all* tell you to use them in the open air."

Carlos said, "Wow, I'm glad that you're so smart! I'll always remember to read the instructions on things I'm using from now on."

Roberto Said No And Came Up With A Better Idea.

Chavis' Story

Chavis and Jesse walked to the corner store to buy a soft drink. There was a cigarette machine by the front door. Jesse said, "Hey, we've got enough money to buy a pack of cigarettes. Let's forget the drinks."

Before you read the next page, answer what you would say or do if you were Chavis:

_____

_____

_____

Chavis' Decision

Chavis knew that cigarettes were dangerous to your health. So he said, "No, I'm really thirsty. I want something to drink."

Jesse said, "Be cool, man. Don't be a chicken."

Chavis said, "No cancer sticks for me. It's your dumb idea. You'll have to smoke them by yourself if you buy them."

Jesse didn't think it was such a cool idea to smoke by himself. There was no one to show off for.

Chavis Returned The Dare.

La Shonda's Story

Vanessa was having a sleepover. She had invited La Shonda. Vanessa's parents had gone to bed. They told the girls that they could stay up until the movie was over.

Vanessa said, "I'm thirsty," and went to the kitchen. When she came back, she had an open bottle of wine in her hand and two glasses.

She said, "My parents have this wine left over from a party. They won't miss just a little."

La Shonda was surprised. What do you think she did? Before you read the next page, answer what you would say or do if you were La Shonda:

_____

_____

_____

La Shonda's Decision

La Shonda laughed and said, "Are you kidding! That stuff will make us turn green!"

But Vanessa was serious. She said, "Come on. Just taste it."

La Shonda said, "No way! I'm hungry. Can I pop some popcorn?" And she walked to the kitchen to find the popcorn. Vanessa came into the kitchen and started helping her. She never mentioned alcohol again.

La Shonda Made A Joke And Came Up With A Better Idea.

Chuy's Story

Chuy and Tad were walking home after school. While passing the high school, they heard the bell ring. Some of the students were hurrying to their cars.

Chuy and Tad noticed that a car had stopped beside them. When they looked to find out who was in it, they saw three high school boys. The older boys said, "Come here. We have something for you."

Chuy and Tad knew who these boys were, and they seemed okay. Tad said, "What do you have?"

"Some grass. You want to smoke some?" they said.

Tad looked at Chuy to make the decision about using marijuana.

Before you read the next page, what would you say or do if you were Chuy?

_____

_____

_____

Chuy's Decision

Chuy knew the answer to smoking marijuana. He said, "I don't smoke grass. I just mow it once a week."

Tad burst out laughing and they walked home together. They knew they didn't want to be dopes. They were **Too Cool for Drugs**.

Chuy Made A Joke And Left.

Chapter 10
Be What
You Want To Be

Maybe I'll be a toy maker
when I grow up.

You can be anything that you want to be when you grow up if you don't use drugs. As you have learned in this book, many drugs are bad for our health. Some drugs even make us unable to drive, to think clearly, or speak clearly. No one would hire anyone like that.

Even though I'm only eight years old, I am dreaming about what I want to be when I grow up. Here are some of my dreams of what I want to be. But I can only reach these dreams if I take good care of my mind and body. Maybe I'll be a…

Teacher

or a...

Thank you, Barbara Sankey, counselor at Carlisle Elementary School, Plano, Texas, for letting Nicholas be teacher for a day.

Dentist

or a...

Thank you, Dr. Byron McKnight, dentist in Mesquite, Texas, for being Nicholas' first patient.

Scientist

or a...

Thank you to Charles McCasland, Principal of Carlisle Elementary School, Plano, Texas, for letting Nicholas explore the science lab.

Mail Carrier

or a...

Thank you, Postmaster John Billimek, Garland, Texas, Post Office, for letting Nicholas help mail carrier Frances Williams deliver the mail.

Professional Athlete

or a...

Nicholas had fun throwing passes to Tony Hill, who played professional football for 10 years for the Dallas Cowboys.

Chiropractor

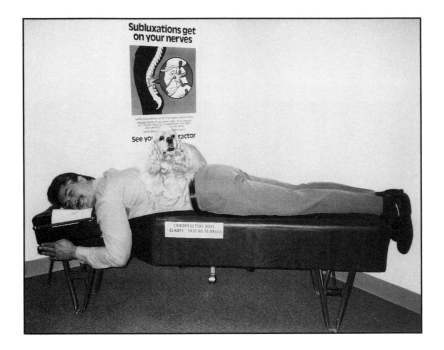

or a...

Our appreciation to Dr. Michael Ashby, chiropractor in Garland, Texas, for trusting Nicholas to adjust his back.

Farmer

or a...

We appreciate Echols Farm Store, Richardson, Texas, for allowing Nicholas to work in their vegetable garden.

Firefighter

or a...

Our appreciation to Chief Bob Wallingford, Town of Addison, Texas, Fire Department, for letting Nicholas fight fires from the antique firetruck on which he rode with firefighters Shara O'Neal and Brian Kanzaki.

Travel Agent

or a...

Thank you to Victoria Campos, travel agent at D-FW Travel Arrangements, Dallas, Texas, for letting Nicholas plan her next vacation.

Pilot

or a...

Nicholas had fun flying the plane owned by Randy Kohltfarber of Plano, Texas. Thank you!

Police Officer

Thank you, Chief James McLaughlin, Town of Addison, Texas, Police Department, for letting Nicholas ride with Officer Peta Reynolds in her patrol car.

What Do You Want To Be When You Grow Up?

Remember not to use drugs so you can keep your mind and body healthy. That way you can be whatever you want to be. Maybe you'll even be…

President

—or Prime Minister—

of your country

I can't believe how much Shawn, Mandy, Cedric, Katy, and I have learned about drugs from Dr. Wayne and Mom. Even Lou Llama learned about drugs. I got a letter from him telling me that he had quit smoking cigarettes. We know we are **Too Cool for Drugs**.

I also know that you are **Too Cool for Drugs**. You now know why not to use drugs. You also know how to turn down drugs.

You are a *very* special person. There is no one else in the world like you. By keeping your mind and body healthy, you can be whatever you want to be. And this world needs you.

Love,

Nicholas

Ending Note to Parents and Teachers

Let *Too Cool for Drugs* be just the beginning of lots of discussion and practice with your child or student.

Suggested ideas:

1. Continue educating yourself on the harmful effects of tobacco, alcohol, and other drugs. New research continues to become available. Share it with the child.

2. When you see a story in the newspaper about someone being injured or dying because of their drug usage, clip it out. Show it to the child.

3. Evaluate your own habits. The "do as I say, not as I do" philosophy just does not work. Children imitate our behaviors. They also worry about our health (and whether we will be around to take care of them). So, if you smoke, make a serious effort to quit. If you drink, watch where you drink (never before or during driving) and how much. If every time you entertain there is alcohol available, you are conveying the message that there is no way to have fun without alcohol. If you reach for a pill every time you get a headache, you are not sending your child a good message. To provide a better example for your child (and a healthier solution for yourself), determine why you have the headache—Have you eaten? Have you sat at your desk too long? Were you reading in low light? Ask yourself questions such as these and try to correct the problem, not the symptom. Use correct terminology (e.g., *alcohol and other drugs; crash,* not accident, when describing a driving-while-intoxicated scene).

4. Teach children to be critical observers of
    commercials and advertisements. They need to know
    that using a certain brand of toothpaste, wearing
    brand-name jeans, smoking cigarettes, drinking
    alcohol, etc. is not what really makes people popular.

5. Write the following organizations concerning
    children's magazines or adult newsletters. All have
    inexpensive membership dues or costs. Each
    provides excellent information:

PRIDE International, Inc.
(Parents' Resource Institute for Drug Education)
10 Park Place South, Suite 340
Atlanta, GA 30303
404-577-4500

PRIDE CANADA, Inc.
College of Pharmacy
University of Saskatchewan
Saskatoon, Saskatchewan S7N0W0
Canada
1-800-667-3747 (within Canada)

**National Federation of Parents
  For Drug-Free Youth**
11159-B South Town Square
St. Louis, MO 63123
314-845-1933

***Winners* Magazine**
The Health Connection
55 W. Oakridge Drive
Hagerstown, MD 21740
1-800-548-8700

***PTA Today* Magazine**
c/o The National PTA
700 North Rush St.
Chicago, IL 60611-2571

There are probably other local, state, or provincial organizations that offer free or inexpensive drug education material. Look them up and call for information.

6. Do a lot more practice using the five ways taught to say no to drugs (See Chapter 9). Set up role-play skits to give the child the opportunity for more practice before a confrontation happens in real life. Tell the child the location of where the skit takes place (e.g., at recess, in the cafeteria, at a sleepover). Then pretend to be the "friend" (but don't use *real* friends' names) who is offering drugs. A skit might look like this:

Parent/Teacher: "Shannon, let's practice being *Too Cool for Drugs*. I'll pretend I'm a friend of yours and we are in the girls' bathroom at school. Think quickly and see if you can decide what to say or do."

Shannon:	"Okay, this will be fun."
Parent/Teacher:	*(reaching into her purse)* "Guess what I have? Let's smoke this cigarette before we have to go back to class."
Shannon:	"No way. Everyone will smell it. And we'll get in trouble."
Parent/Teacher:	"We won't get caught. I thought you were my friend."
Shannon:	"I am your friend. But I'm not going to smoke a cigarette with you. I'm going back to class." *(She turns to leave.)*
Parent/Teacher:	"Shannon, that was excellent! You used three ways to say no to drugs. What were they?"
Shannon:	"I said, 'No,' returned the dare, and walkcd away."
Parent/Teacher:	"I am so proud of you. You are *Too Cool for Drugs.*"

These skits can be practiced most anywhere, including:

1. At home

2. In class

3. In the car to or from school

4. At scout meetings

5. With neighborhood practice groups of children and parents

6. By having the child teach, with your help, a younger sibling or student.

The point is, of course, that the more practice children have, the less likely they are to be puzzled by what to say or do when pressured to do drugs. (For more information and practice on refusal skills to all kinds of peer-invited trouble—not just drugs— you may want to get Sharon Scott's grade K-4 book, *Too Smart for Trouble*. See page 120.)

7. Have your child or student write a letter to Nicholas and tell him what they learned in *Too Cool for Drugs*. Nicholas has his own stationery and always answers his mail! His address is the same as Sharon Scott's (see page 119).

Dr. Wayne Hindmarsh is available as a resource to parents and helping professionals in these areas:

- The Health Consequences of Drug Use
- Drugs and Alcohol In the Workplace
- Alcohol: A Major Problem for Minors
- The ABCs of Inhalant Use
- PRIDE: A Partial Solution to the Drug Problem

Write for further information:

Wayne Hindmarsh, Ph.D., Dean
Faculty of Pharmacy
The University of Manitoba
Winnipeg, Manitoba R3T2N2
Canada

Sharon Scott is available in the following capacities:

- Keynote or workshop leader for adults, teens, or children on many topics, including *Too Cool for Drugs*
- Implementing peer-helping groups
- Inservice for teachers and counselors on **Peer Pressure Reversal: Survival Skills for the '90s**, and other topics
- "Positive Parenting" column for newsletters
- Teen video, "Like a Roaring Lion"

Write or call for further information:

Sharon Scott and Associates (and Nicholas)
2709 Woods Lane
Garland, Texas 75044-2807
214-495-3477

Contact:

Human Resource Development Press
22 Amherst Rd.
Amherst, MA 01002
U.S.A.
1-800-822-2801 (U.S. and Canada)
413-253-3488 (within Massachusetts
    and other countries)

for information on ordering Sharon Scott's books:

- *Peer Pressure Reversal: An Adult Guide to Developing a Responsible Child*

- *How to Say No and Keep Your Friends* (grades 5-12)

- *Too Smart for Trouble* (grades K-4)

- *Positive Peer Groups* (adults)

- *When to Say Yes! And Make More Friends* (grades 5-12)

- *Not Better... Not Worse... Just Different* (grades K-4)

- *Too Cool for Drugs* (grades 1-5)

Discounts given on quantity orders. Call for details.

Also available are teaching transparencies on all three of Nicholas' books and a 14″ Nicholas hand puppet to use as teaching resources.